New Zealand
Travel Guide 2024

A Comprehensive Guide to 2024's Kiwi Marvels

Amanda Fenner

Copyright © 2023 by Amanda Fenner

All rights reserved. No part of this publication may be reproduced, distributed, or transmitted in any form or by any means, including photocopying, recording, or other electronic or mechanical methods, without the prior written permission of the publisher, except in the case of brief quotations embodied in critical reviews and certain other noncommercial uses permitted by copyright law.

This guide is intended for informational purposes only. The author and publisher make no representations or warranties with respect to the accuracy or completeness of the contents of this work and specifically disclaim all warranties, including without limitation warranties of fitness for a particular purpose. The advice and strategies contained herein may not be suitable for every situation. The author and publisher shall not be liable for any damages arising from the use of or reliance on this guide.

Table of Contents

- Introduction 6
  - Welcome to Kiwi Paradise 6
  - What's New in 2024 8
- Getting Started 11
  - Planning Your Trip 11
  - Visa Information 12
  - Budgeting and Currency Tips 12
- Navigating New Zealand 14
  - Regions and Highlights 15
  - Transportation Guide 16
  - Weather and Best Times to Visit 17
- Cultural Immersion 18
  - Maori Traditions and Etiquette 18
  - Festivals and Events in 2024 19
  - Local Customs and Traditions 20
- Natural Wonders 22
  - Fiordland National Park 22
  - Tongariro Alpine Crossing 23
  - Abel Tasman Coastal Track 25
- City Escapes 28
  - Auckland: City of Sails 28
  - Wellington: Capital Cool 30

Christchurch: Garden City Reimagined... 32
Culinary Delights.. 36
    Kiwi Cuisine Overview... 36
    Must-Try Dishes... 37
    Food Festivals in 2024.. 39
Accommodation Guide... 41
    Hotels, Hostels, and Unique Stays... 41
    Booking Tips.. 43
Sustainable Travel... 45
    Eco-Friendly Practices... 45
    Responsible Tourism Tips.. 47
Useful Resources... 50
    Language basics... 52
    Packing Checklist:... 52
Map Of New Zealand.. 55
Conclusion.. 56
    Reflecting on Your Kiwi Adventure.. 56
    Share Your Experience.. 57
Love from Author.. 59

Introduction

Welcome to Kiwi Paradise

Greetings fellow adventurer! I'm Amanda Fenner, and I'm delighted to serve as your companion on a journey through the captivating landscapes and dynamic culture of New Zealand in 2024. This travel companion is more than a mere compilation of information; it extends a personal invitation to uncover the enchantment concealed in every nook of this Kiwi haven.

As you peruse these pages, envision yourself standing on the shores of the immaculate Milford Sound, surrounded by towering cliffs and cascading waterfalls. Experience the exhilaration of bungee jumping in Queenstown, renowned as the adventure capital of the world. Envision the tranquil beauty of the Abel Tasman Coastal Track, where golden beaches meet luxuriant rainforests.

Yet, this guide transcends being a visual spectacle; it serves as a roadmap to tailor your unique Kiwi experience. Whether you're an adrenaline junkie, a cultural aficionado, or a gastronomic enthusiast, New Zealand has something extraordinary crafted just for you. Immerse yourself in the rich traditions of the Maori people, partake in lively festivals, and relish the distinctive flavors of Kiwi cuisine.

For me, exploring New Zealand transcends ticking off landmarks; it involves immersing oneself in the essence of each region. Auckland, with its iconic skyline and maritime culture, Wellington, a city seamlessly blending art and history, and Christchurch, rising from the ruins with a reimagined spirit – these cities aren't just dots on a map but living narratives eager to be lived.

As we traverse this awe-inspiring land, I'll provide insights on responsible travel and ways to connect with local communities. Let's not merely visit New Zealand; let's integrate ourselves into it, leaving behind only footprints and carrying memories destined to endure a lifetime.

So, intrepid traveler, secure your seatbelt or tighten your hiking boots – your Kiwi escapade commences right here, within the pages of this guide. Prepare to script your own tale in the heart of New Zealand – an authentic haven for wanderers.

What's New in 2024

Ahoy there, fellow explorers! Amanda Fenner at your service, serving as your reliable companion on the Kiwi journey unfolding in 2024. Fasten your seatbelts for a ride into the freshest and finest experiences awaiting you in the captivating world of New Zealand.

As we embark on the voyage into a new year, New Zealand is abuzz with anticipation and novel encounters. Envision this: avant-garde environmentally conscious initiatives, cutting-edge advancements in travel technology, and a revitalized dedication to sustainable tourism. In 2024, the allure of the Kiwi paradise extends beyond its awe-inspiring landscapes; it's about embracing a more environmentally conscious and mindful approach to exploration.

For those seeking an adrenaline rush, brace yourself for heart-pounding additions to the adventure landscape. Queenstown, famed for its bungee jumping, unveils exhilarating activities that will send your heart racing and your enthusiasm soaring. Prepare for the unexpected – New Zealand isn't just a destination; it's an ever-changing playground for the spirited adventurer.

Culture enthusiasts, gear up for an immersive expedition into the core of Maori traditions. In 2024, festivals and events illuminate the vibrant tapestry of New Zealand's indigenous culture. Experience the beat of the haka, partake in traditional feasts, and witness ceremonies that have endured through time. The past and present harmonize in a jubilation that invites you to become a part of the living history of Aotearoa.

Yet, it's not solely about heart-pounding adventures and culturally enriching escapades; culinary aficionados are in for a delectable treat. New Zealand's gastronomic scene is undergoing a renaissance, with inventive chefs blending traditional flavors with global influences. Roam through farmers' markets, relish farm-to-table dining, and savor the distinct gastronomic odyssey that Kiwi cuisine unfolds.

So, what's the scoop in 2024? It transcends mere locations; it's about the evolving essence of New Zealand. Join me on this expedition, where every instant captures the essence of the present and provides a peek into the thrilling future of Kiwi exploration.

Getting Started

Planning Your Trip

Embarking on your Kiwi journey commences with meticulous planning. New Zealand, with its captivating array of landscapes and cultural richness, requires a carefully crafted itinerary. Start by identifying your passions – whether you're drawn to the serene beauty of Fiordland National Park, seeking thrills in Queenstown, or eager to delve into Maori traditions as a culture aficionado. Let your interests shape the course of your adventure.

Account for the seasons; New Zealand's weather is as varied as its terrain. Whether you crave the warmth of summer or the snowy embrace of winter, understanding the climate is crucial. Develop a flexible itinerary, allowing room for unexpected discoveries and impromptu detours that can turn your journey into an extraordinary experience.

Research becomes your ally in shaping the perfect adventure. Delve into local blogs, travel forums, and the latest travel apps to tap into the collective wisdom of fellow explorers. Dive deep into each destination, uncovering hidden gems and off-the-beaten-path wonders. Let your curiosity drive your research, revealing not just tourist spots but the soul of each location.

Visa Information

Navigating the bureaucratic landscape is an inherent part of international travel, and New Zealand is no exception. Familiarize yourself with visa requirements well in advance to ensure a smooth entry. The New Zealand immigration website is a goldmine of information, guiding you through visa types, application processes, and any recent updates.

For some countries, New Zealand has implemented electronic travel authorizations, streamlining the entry process. Stay abreast of the latest developments and alterations in visa policies, ensuring your documents are in order for a seamless entry.

Budgeting and Currency Tips

Finances play a pivotal role, and a well-thought-out budget is the foundation of any successful trip. Begin by outlining your overall travel budget, encompassing accommodation, transportation, activities, and meals. New Zealand caters to various budgets, from backpacker hostels to luxury lodges, allowing you to customize expenses based on your preferences.

Consider exchange rates and be mindful of fluctuating currency values. While ATMs are widespread, it's prudent to carry a mix of cash and cards, especially in more remote areas. Budgeting is not merely about saving; it's about allocating resources effectively to maximize experiences.

Explore local markets and eateries to relish the authentic flavors of Kiwi cuisine without straining your budget. Immerse yourself in the vibrant food culture, from beachside fish and chips to farmers' market treasures. Exploring on a budget doesn't mean sacrificing experiences; it means uncovering the genuine essence of New Zealand without unnecessary frills.

In the spirit of our agreement, this guide is tailored for you to seamlessly infuse your own voice and preferences. Customize the details to your liking, adding personal touches that transform this comprehensive guide into your unique travel companion. So, let the planning begin – your Kiwi adventure awaits!

Navigating New Zealand

Embarking on a voyage through the heart of New Zealand promises an exploration teeming with marvels awaiting discovery. In this section, let's delve into the intricacies of navigating this Kiwi haven, unveiling the diverse regions and highlights that transform each nook of the nation into a distinctive tapestry of experiences.

Regions and Highlights

The allure of New Zealand resides in its geographical variety, and grasping the unique attributes of each region is the gateway to an authentically immersive journey. The North Island, adorned with geothermal marvels, verdant forests, and lively urban hubs, mesmerizes with its vibrant vitality.

Auckland, renowned as the City of Sails, greets visitors with its iconic skyline and a bustling waterfront. Immerse yourself in the cultural mosaic of Wellington, the nation's capital, where art and history entwine in an enchanting dance. The Bay of Islands, boasting pristine beaches and historic sites, extends an invitation to relax in a tropical paradise.

The South Island, a haven for nature enthusiasts, showcases rugged landscapes, majestic fjords, and alpine marvels. Fiordland National Park, housing the iconic Milford Sound, is a symphony of towering peaks and cascading waterfalls. Queenstown, the adventure capital, lures thrill-seekers with bungee jumping and other heart-pounding activities.

The West Coast, with its untamed wilderness, unveils the beauty of Punakaiki's Pancake Rocks and the Franz Josef Glacier. In the east, the charming town of Kaikoura offers a unique blend of marine life encounters and stunning coastal vistas. Each region narrates a distinctive chapter of New Zealand's narrative, and exploring them is akin to turning the pages of an enthralling novel.

Transportation Guide

Traversing New Zealand's diverse terrains is an adventure in itself, and a well-planned transportation strategy ensures a seamless journey. Opting for car rentals provides the freedom to explore at your own pace, allowing you to stray from the conventional path and uncover hidden treasures. The winding roads of the South Island offer breathtaking views at every turn, transforming the journey into an integral part of the overall experience.

For those desiring a more laid-back approach, the comprehensive bus and coach network links major cities and regions, offering a scenic route with the luxury of sitting back and savoring the view. Domestic flights serve as a time-efficient option, connecting key destinations and offering a bird's-eye perspective of the diverse terrain below.

Ferry crossings, such as the iconic journey between the North and South Islands, provide a maritime adventure with sweeping views of the Cook Strait. Embrace the diversity of transportation options to curate a journey that aligns with your preferences, allowing you to relish every moment of the Kiwi landscape.

Weather and Best Times to Visit

New Zealand's climate mirrors its landscapes in diversity, and discerning the seasonal nuances elevates the quality of your adventure. Summer, from December to February, bathes the country in warmth, making it an ideal time for outdoor pursuits and beach retreats. Autumn introduces a palette of rich hues, creating a picturesque backdrop for exploration.

Winter, from June to August, blankets the Southern Alps in snow, beckoning skiing and snowboarding enthusiasts to the alpine resorts. Spring, from September to November, witnesses nature's reawakening with blooming flowers and newborn wildlife. Each season paints a unique canvas, and the ideal time to visit hinges on your preferred activities and climate inclinations.

In the North Island, the shoulder seasons of spring and autumn offer agreeable temperatures and fewer crowds. The South Island's winter transforms its alpine regions into a winter wonderland, attracting snow enthusiasts. Plan your visit based on the experiences you crave, whether it's sun-soaked adventures, autumnal hikes, or snowy escapades.

As you navigate New Zealand's diverse regions, transportation modes, and weather patterns, allow the journey to unfold like a finely crafted narrative. Each chapter reveals a fresh facet of this Kiwi tale, inviting you to immerse yourself in the rich tapestry of experiences that renders New Zealand a destination unparalleled in its uniqueness.

Cultural Immersion

Embarking on a New Zealand expedition goes beyond mere admiration of its landscapes; it's an opportunity to unravel the intricate tapestry of its cultural legacy. This section will delve into the art of cultural integration, exploring Maori traditions and engaging in the lively festivals that epitomize the spirit of 2024.

Maori Traditions and Etiquette

To authentically connect with the heart of New Zealand, an exploration of Maori traditions becomes imperative. The Maori, New Zealand's indigenous Polynesian population, possess a cultural heritage intricately woven into the fabric of the land. When interacting with Maori communities, observance of their customs becomes paramount.

The traditional Maori salutation, the hongi, entails the gentle pressing of noses and foreheads, symbolizing the exchange of life's breath and extending goodwill. Embrace this practice with sincerity, showcasing a genuine desire to forge a deeper connection.

Grasping the significance of the haka, a potent ceremonial dance, adds another dimension to cultural immersion. The haka serves as a visceral expression of Maori identity, employed to welcome guests, acknowledge accomplishments, and pay homage to the departed. Witnessing or participating in a haka performance is a profound and emotional encounter, offering insight into the resilience and unity of the Maori people.

Festivals and Events in 2024

In 2024, New Zealand's calendar is replete with festivals and events that illuminate the nation's creativity, diversity, and zest for life. The biennial Te Matatini Kapa Haka Festival, the epitome of Maori performing arts, guarantees a captivating showcase of song and dance. Immerse yourself in the rhythm and vitality of this cultural spectacle, where tribes from across the country unite to celebrate their heritage.

The Auckland Arts Festival metamorphoses the city into a dynamic center of creativity, featuring a spectrum of performances, exhibitions, and cultural happenings. From contemporary dance to traditional Maori art, the festival stands as a testament to the thriving arts scene in New Zealand.

For enthusiasts of gastronomy, the Wild Food Festival in Hokitika is an unparalleled culinary odyssey. Indulge in unconventional culinary delights, from huhu grubs to whitebait fritters, and experience the fusion of traditional and contemporary Kiwi cuisine.

Local Customs and Traditions

New Zealand's allure lies not only in its natural marvels but also in the everyday practices that mold its distinct identity. Kiwis, affectionately known as New Zealanders, are renowned for their amiability and hospitality. Engage in casual exchanges with locals, whether at a café, on public transportation, or during community events. The warmth of the people adds an authentic layer to your cultural immersion.

Participate in the "shout" tradition at a local pub. The shout entails one person treating the group to a round of drinks, fostering a convivial atmosphere of camaraderie. Embrace this gesture of generosity and reciprocate in kind, establishing connections within the Kiwi community.

Respect for the environment is deeply ingrained in Kiwi culture, and responsible tourism aligns with local values. Dispose of waste conscientiously, support eco-friendly initiatives, and tread lightly in natural areas to leave behind a positive footprint.

Cultural engagement in New Zealand extends beyond observation, urging active participation in the traditions that define this island nation. Whether partaking in the hongi, reveling in festival festivities, or adopting local customs, let each encounter paint a unique stroke on the canvas of your Kiwi adventure, creating memories that resonate long after your journey concludes.

Natural Wonders

Embarking on a voyage across New Zealand is a plunge into a world of natural marvels that enrapture the spirit. From the towering summits of the Southern Alps to the unspoiled shorelines tracing the coast, every nook of this Kiwi haven speaks to the breathtaking beauty of nature. In the following passages, we'll delve into the captivating terrains of Fiordland National Park, the compelling charm of the Tongariro Alpine Crossing, and the coastal magnificence of the Abel Tasman Coastal Track.

Fiordland National Park

Nestled in the southwestern corner of the South Island, Fiordland National Park stands as a living testament to the untamed beauty of New Zealand's wilderness, acknowledged as a UNESCO World Heritage Site. Sculpted by ancient glaciers, Fiordland is an artwork of fiords, waterfalls, and towering cliffs.

The gem of Fiordland, Milford Sound, demands attention with its sheer magnificence. Cruising through the tranquil waters, one is humbled by the towering Mitre Peak and surrounded by cascading waterfalls, such as the iconic Lady Bowen Falls. The interplay of light on the cliffs and the peaks' reflections in the water compose a visual poetry both humbling and exhilarating.

Doubtful Sound, another treasure concealed within Fiordland, offers a secluded and unspoiled encounter. Accessible by boat or kayak, this fiord immerses visitors in the tranquility of ancient rainforests and the haunting beauty of granite walls rising from the water.

For the adventurous, Fiordland is a haven of hiking trails leading to panoramic viewpoints. The Kepler Track and the Routeburn Track traverse diverse landscapes, providing a comprehensive immersion into the ecological richness of the park, from moss-draped forests to alpine meadows.

Fiordland National Park narrates the geological story of New Zealand's topography. Each fiord, waterfall, and towering peak whispers the tale of the earth's profound artistry, inviting observers to witness an ongoing masterpiece.

Tongariro Alpine Crossing

Journeying to the heart of the North Island, the Tongariro Alpine Crossing unfolds as a trek through a landscape seemingly borrowed from a fantastical realm. Nestled within Tongariro National Park, a dual UNESCO World Heritage Site, this crossing is an exploration of the dynamic forces that shaped New Zealand.

Often lauded as one of the world's greatest day hikes, the trail winds through a surreal landscape dominated by volcanic peaks, craters, and vibrant emerald lakes. Ascending the steep slopes of the Red Crater, panoramic views, including Mount Ngauruhoe (known as Mount Doom from "The Lord of the Rings" trilogy), take one's breath away.

The trail traverses the otherworldly South Crater, surrounded by volcanic ridges, before descending into the ethereal beauty of the Emerald Lakes. Tinted by minerals leaching from the thermal area, these lakes create a mesmerizing and alien visual spectacle.

The descent leads through alpine meadows and tussock-covered slopes, showcasing nature's resilience as alpine plants cling to life amidst the harsh volcanic environment.

The Tongariro Alpine Crossing is not just a physical journey; it's a pilgrimage through a living geological gallery. It's an opportunity to walk in the footsteps of ancient forces and witness the ever-changing face of the earth beneath your feet.

Abel Tasman Coastal Track

On the northern tip of the South Island, the Abel Tasman Coastal Track unfolds as a sun-drenched paradise where golden beaches meet the turquoise embrace of the Tasman Sea. This coastal track is a sensory journey, a tapestry of landscapes blending lush forests, pristine beaches, and the rhythmic melody of lapping waves.

Stretching 60 kilometers along Abel Tasman National Park, New Zealand's smallest but most captivating national park, the journey can be as leisurely or adventurous as desired. The scent of native flora permeates the air as you wander through ancient beech forests, creating an immersive experience.

The allure lies in secluded bays and coves like Anchorage, Torrent Bay, and Bark Bay, each more enchanting than the last. These spots beckon with golden sands, providing idyllic locations for a refreshing dip in the crystal-clear waters. Kayaking is a popular choice for exploring the coastline, navigating hidden sea caves and marveling at diverse marine life.

A unique feature is the low tide coastal crossing at Awaroa Inlet. Wade through shallow waters and witness the interplay of light and shadows on the sandy seabed – a moment adding a touch of adventure to your coastal odyssey.

As the day wanes, the sunset transforms the landscape into a canvas of warm hues, casting a magical glow over the golden beaches. Camping under the southern hemisphere stars, with the rhythmic sounds of the ocean as a lullaby, completes the sensory symphony of the Abel Tasman Coastal Track.

Traversing the Abel Tasman Coastal Track is more than hiking; it's participating in a dance with nature. Each step reveals a new coastal panorama, and each bay promises serenity and discovery. It's a coastal journey inviting you to slow down, breathe in the salty air, and lose yourself in the timeless beauty of New Zealand's coastal masterpiece.

Embarking on the trails of Fiordland National Park, the Tongariro Alpine Crossing, and the Abel Tasman Coastal Track is not merely a physical journey; it's a pilgrimage through the diverse landscapes that define New Zealand's natural wonders. These are not just hiking trails; they are narratives written by the earth, inviting you to be an active participant in the unfolding story of this Kiwi paradise.

City Escapes

Embarking on a New Zealand odyssey is not just a venture into its natural wonders; it's a plunge into the dynamic urban panoramas that shape the cultural pulse of this island realm. In this section, we'll meander through the urban retreats of Auckland, the City of Sails; Wellington, the Capital Cool; and Christchurch, the Garden City Reimagined. Each city spins its own tale, fusing contemporary flair with tradition, weaving a distinctive tapestry that enriches the Kiwi experience.

Auckland: City of Sails

Auckland, New Zealand's sprawling metropolis, stretches across a narrow isthmus between the Tasman Sea and the Pacific Ocean, earning the moniker "City of Sails." This lively city seamlessly merges urban refinement with the awe-inspiring beauty of its surrounding harbors and isles.

Commence your Auckland journey with a visit to the iconic Sky Tower, the Southern Hemisphere's tallest freestanding structure. Ascend to the observation deck for sweeping views, extending from the cityscape to the distant horizons of the Hauraki Gulf. For the adventurous, the SkyJump and SkyWalk offer exhilarating exploits, elevating your urban escapade.

Auckland's waterfront is a hub of activity, with the Viaduct Harbour at its core—a nexus of dining, entertainment, and maritime allure. Saunter along the water's edge, taking in luxury yachts and relishing waterfront dining against the backdrop of city lights.

For a dose of culture, the Auckland Art Gallery Toi o Tāmaki houses a diverse collection of New Zealand and global art. Roam through contemporary exhibitions and Maori artifacts, gaining insight into the artistic legacy that defines the nation.

Escape the urban hustle with a ferry voyage to Waiheke Island, a sanctuary of vineyards, beaches, and artistic endeavors. The island's laid-back atmosphere provides a stark contrast to Auckland's energetic rhythm, offering a glimpse into the multifaceted character of New Zealand's largest city.

Auckland is not just a city; it's a maritime masterpiece where the urban tapestry twirls with the ebb and flow of surrounding waters. From towering structures to tranquil islands, Auckland beckons you to savor the harmonious fusion of cosmopolitan vitality and maritime serenity.

Wellington: Capital Cool

Nestled at the southern tip of the North Island, Wellington, the capital city, exudes an air of cool sophistication that resonates with its vibrant cultural milieu. Surrounded by hills and the cerulean waters of Wellington Harbour, the city offers an intimate and captivating urban retreat.

Embark on your Wellington adventure with a trip to Te Papa Tongarewa, the national museum of New Zealand. This cultural hub delves into the nation's history, art, and natural heritage, presenting interactive exhibits and immersive displays that encapsulate the essence of Kiwi identity.

Wellington's waterfront is a dynamic canvas where creativity flourishes. The Wellington Waterfront Sculpture Trail invites you to explore a curated collection of contemporary artworks against the backdrop of the harbor. Oriental Bay beach, with its golden sands and azure waters, provides a picturesque setting for leisurely strolls and water activities.

For a touch of nostalgia, board the Wellington Cable Car, an iconic funicular ascending from Lambton Quay to Kelburn. The summit's panoramic views encompass the cityscape, harbor, and distant hills, offering a unique perspective of Wellington's terrain.

Wellington's coffee culture thrives, with eclectic cafes dotting the city where baristas craft artisanal brews. Wander through Cuba Street, a bohemian enclave adorned with street art, boutique shops, and a lively ambiance—an alluring spot for both locals and visitors.

Wellington's film industry prowess shines at the Weta Workshop, a creative studio famed for its contributions to "The Lord of the Rings" and other blockbusters. Take a guided tour to witness the artistry behind the movie magic, gaining insights into prop making and special effects.

Wellington is more than a political hub; it's a cultural oasis where creativity flourishes, and chicness is ingrained in its identity. From artistic expressions to scenic panoramas, the capital city invites you to delve into the multifaceted layers that make Wellington a captivating urban escape.

Christchurch: Garden City Reimagined

Nestled on the east coast of the South Island, Christchurch, the largest city in the South Island, is a saga of resilience and rebirth. Emerging as a symbol of community strength after the devastating earthquakes of 2010 and 2011, the city seamlessly blends the old with the new in a reimaged garden city.

Embark on your Christchurch exploration at the Botanic Gardens, a verdant oasis in the city's heart. Stroll through curated landscapes, including the enchanting Rose Garden and tranquil Canterbury Gardens.

Punting on the Avon River offers a leisurely and picturesque way to experience the gardens from a different perspective.

The Christchurch Art Gallery Te Puna o Waiwhetū exemplifies the city's dedication to the arts. Showcasing a diverse collection of contemporary and traditional artworks, the gallery serves as a platform for local and international artists. The building itself is an architectural marvel, inviting exploration of its light-filled spaces and engaging exhibitions.

Adjacent to the Botanic Gardens, the Canterbury Museum delves into the natural and cultural history of the region. From Maori artifacts to Antarctic explorations, the museum provides a comprehensive journey through the stories shaping Christchurch and its environs.

The Christchurch Cathedral, an emblem for over a century, underwent significant restoration post-earthquakes. While the iconic spire no longer graces the skyline, the cathedral's reimagined form stands as a testament to the city's commitment to preserving its heritage while embracing a new era.

The Cardboard Cathedral, a temporary structure constructed from cardboard tubes, showcases Christchurch's innovative spirit. Conceived as a transitional space during the original cathedral's restoration, this architectural marvel underscores the city's ability to turn adversity into opportunity.

Christchurch's revitalization extends to its culinary scene, with the vibrant Riverside Market offering a gastronomic adventure. From artisanal treats to international flavors, the market is a melting pot of culinary delights. The adjacent Avon River Precinct, with its pedestrian-friendly paths and public spaces, beckons you to savor the city's renewed vibrancy.

Christchurch is not merely a city; it's a narrative of transformation and renewal. From lush gardens to architectural innovations, the city invites you to witness its journey of resilience and reimagination. Each step through Christchurch is a testament to the indomitable spirit that defines the Garden City in its new chapter.

In navigating the urban realms of Auckland, Wellington, and Christchurch, you're not just traversing cityscapes; you're immersing yourself in the cultural rhythm of New Zealand. From Auckland's maritime grandeur to Wellington's creative coolness and Christchurch's resilient revival, each city escape weaves a distinctive tale, inviting you to become an integral part of its narrative.

Culinary Delights

Embarking on a voyage through New Zealand unveils not only a spectacular visual panorama but also an epicurean odyssey that exposes the rich and diverse tapestry of Kiwi cuisine. From the traditional Maori essence to modern culinary amalgamations, New Zealand's gastronomic landscape mirrors the captivating beauty of its terrains. In this section, let's relish the gastronomic wonders of Kiwi cuisine, discover the essential dishes, and highlight the upcoming food festivals that promise to delight taste buds in 2024.

Kiwi Cuisine Overview

Kiwi cuisine mirrors the geographical diversity of the nation, blending fresh, locally sourced ingredients into a culinary repertoire spanning from the earth to the ocean. The culinary ethos revolves around honoring the inherent flavors of ingredients, resulting in dishes that are both delectable and nourishing.

Seafood commands a prominent role in Kiwi cuisine, owing to the abundant coastal waters of New Zealand. Green-lipped mussels, Bluff oysters, and succulent crayfish grace seafood menus, showcasing the pristine flavors of the surrounding oceans. New Zealand takes the concept of "surf and turf" to new heights, where the bounty of the sea meets the richness of pasture-fed meats.

Lamb, a Kiwi favorite, is renowned for its tenderness and succulence. The lush pastures contribute to the superior quality of lamb, often prepared with simple yet flavorful seasonings that allow the natural taste of the meat to shine.

Influences from the indigenous Maori culture are evident in the widespread use of kumara (sweet potato), fern shoots, and native herbs. The Maori hangi, a traditional earth oven cooking method, imparts a distinctive smokiness to meats and vegetables, offering a unique sensory experience.

Contemporary Kiwi cuisine embraces innovation, with chefs incorporating global influences into traditional dishes. Fusion restaurants and establishments experimenting with molecular gastronomy are on the rise, injecting a modern twist into the culinary landscape.

Must-Try Dishes

Embarking on a culinary expedition through New Zealand invites you to a passport of unique, bold, and distinctly Kiwi flavors. Here are some essential dishes that guarantee to tantalize your taste buds:

> **Pavlova**: A regal dessert, pavlova features a meringue base adorned with fresh fruits, often kiwi, and drizzled with passion fruit. The crisp exterior and soft, pillowy interior create a harmonious interplay of textures.
>
> **Hangi**: Immerse yourself in Maori tradition with a hangi feast. Meats, vegetables, and sometimes seafood are slow-cooked in an

earth oven, resulting in tender, smoky flavors that pay homage to indigenous cooking methods.

Paua Fritters: Paua, a type of abalone, is a New Zealand delicacy. Paua fritters, made by battering and frying thinly sliced paua, offer a taste of the ocean with a satisfying crunch.

Whitebait: These tiny, translucent fish are a Kiwi delicacy, often enjoyed in a simple whitebait fritter. Minimal seasoning preserves the delicate flavor, allowing the natural essence to shine.

Kumara Chips: Move over regular fries; kumara chips are a sweet and savory revelation. Sliced kumara is fried to crispy perfection, offering a delightful alternative to traditional potato chips.

Hokey Pokey Ice Cream: Indulge your sweet tooth with hokey pokey ice cream, a classic Kiwi treat. Vanilla ice cream studded with crunchy, honeycomb-like toffee creates a textural symphony that's as delightful as it is delicious.

Feijoa: This tropical fruit, reminiscent of guava and pineapple, is a Kiwi favorite. Enjoy it fresh or in desserts, adding a burst of tropical sweetness to your palate.

Food Festivals in 2024

In 2024, New Zealand's food festivals promise a culinary journey, celebrating the country's diverse culinary offerings. From seafood extravaganzas to wine and food pairings, these festivals invite you to savor the best of Kiwi cuisine. Mark your calendars for these culinary celebrations:

Marlborough Wine and Food Festival (February): Celebrate the region's renowned Sauvignon Blanc and other varietals amidst vineyards, with wine tastings, gourmet food stalls, and live entertainment.

Wild Food Festival, Hokitika (March): Adventure awaits at this festival, where exotic dishes like huhu grubs, whitebait fritters, and wild game are sampled in a festive atmosphere filled with live music and entertainment.

Auckland Seafood Festival (January): Auckland's waterfront comes alive with the flavors of the sea, offering fresh oysters to grilled fish, along with live music and entertainment.

Wellington on a Plate (August): This culinary extravaganza in the capital city celebrates Wellington's vibrant food scene with fine dining, street food, special menus, food tours, and competitions.

Hawke's Bay Food and Wine Classic (F.A.W.C!) (June/November): Set in picturesque Hawke's Bay, F.A.W.C! showcases local produce, wine, and culinary talent through winery tours, themed dinners, and masterclasses.

South Island Wine and Food Festival, Christchurch (December): As the year concludes, Christchurch hosts a festival highlighting the South

Island's finest wines and local fare, complemented by live music and entertainment.

Participating in these food festivals goes beyond indulging in delectable dishes; it's a cultural and culinary immersion, allowing you to connect with the essence of Kiwi flavors and the communities that shape them.

In savoring the culinary treasures of New Zealand, you're not merely enjoying a meal; you're embarking on a sensory voyage that mirrors the nation's diverse landscapes and cultural influences. From traditional Maori culinary delights to contemporary innovations, Kiwi cuisine is a celebration of freshness, flavor, and ingenuity. As you explore the must-try dishes and mark your calendar for upcoming food festivals, you're poised to embark on a gastronomic adventure that will leave an indelible mark on your Kiwi experience.

Accommodation Guide

Embarking on a journey through the captivating landscapes of New Zealand necessitates finding the perfect accommodation to guarantee a comfortable and unforgettable experience. This guide delves into the myriad accommodation options, spanning luxurious hotels, budget-friendly hostels, and distinctive stays that infuse a touch of Kiwi charm. Additionally, we offer tips for booking to help you navigate the extensive choices and secure the ideal abode for your adventure.

Hotels, Hostels, and Unique Stays

Hotels: Merging Luxury with Kiwi Splendor

New Zealand presents a spectrum of hotels catering to diverse tastes and preferences. From lavish lodges nestled in nature's heart to chic urban retreats, the Kiwi paradise's hotel scene is characterized by its diversity.

Luxury lodges, like those in Queenstown or Rotorua, provide not just opulent accommodations but immersive experiences. Imagine waking up to panoramic mountain views or indulging in a spa retreat surrounded by native bush, seamlessly blending with the natural surroundings to create an oasis of tranquility.

Urban hotels, especially in cities like Auckland and Wellington, offer a different form of luxury. With world-class amenities, fine dining, and proximity to cultural attractions, these hotels ensure a seamless blend of comfort and convenience for discerning travelers.

Hostels: Affordable Retreats for Social Explorers

For budget-conscious or socially inclined travelers, New Zealand's hostels are an excellent option. Beyond affordable accommodations, these hostels offer a vibrant and friendly atmosphere, providing opportunities to connect with fellow global travelers.

Major cities and popular backpacker destinations, such as Queenstown and Taupo, boast a variety of hostels catering to different preferences. Whether you prefer a communal dormitory setting or a private room, hostels foster a laid-back environment with shared kitchens and common areas, promoting a sense of camaraderie.

Unique Stays: Infusing Kiwi Quirkiness into Your Journey

New Zealand's distinctive charm extends to its accommodation options, allowing travelers to stay in unconventional and memorable spaces. From treehouse retreats in the Bay of Islands to cozy cabins with scenic views, these unique stays amplify the Kiwi experience.

Consider immersing yourself in a traditional Maori marae (meeting house) for a culturally rich encounter. Alternatively, indulge in stargazing from a glamping site in the Mackenzie Basin, where luxury meets the rugged beauty of the night sky.

Booking Tips

Plan Ahead, Especially in Peak Seasons:
New Zealand's popularity peaks during certain times, such as the summer months (December to February). To secure your preferred accommodation, especially in high-demand areas, planning and booking well in advance is advisable.

Explore Online Reviews and Ratings:
Utilize online platforms and review websites to gain insights into the quality and reputation of accommodations. Real traveler reviews often offer valuable information about comfort, cleanliness, and overall experiences.

Consider Location in Relation to Activities:
With diverse attractions in New Zealand, your choice of accommodation can enhance your overall experience. Whether exploring cities, engaging in outdoor adventures, or immersing yourself in cultural activities, consider your accommodation's location in relation to planned activities.

Budget vs. Amenities:
Define your priorities regarding budget and amenities. If on a tighter budget, plentiful hostels and budget-friendly options are available. For a more luxurious experience, investing in well-appointed hotels or unique stays may be worthwhile.

Take Advantage of Loyalty Programs and Deals:
Many hotel chains and booking platforms offer loyalty programs or exclusive deals for frequent travelers. Signing up for newsletters,

memberships, or loyalty programs can provide access to special discounts or perks during your stay.

Read Booking Policies Carefully:
Before confirming your reservation, carefully review booking policies, including cancellation fees and refund options. Flexibility is crucial, especially when travel plans may be subject to change.

Embrace Local Hospitality:
Consider accommodations that showcase Kiwi hospitality, such as bed and breakfasts, boutique lodges, and family-run establishments. These not only offer personalized experiences but also provide an opportunity to connect with the local community.

Utilize Booking Platforms and Apps:
Take advantage of online booking platforms and mobile apps like Booking.com, Airbnb, and Expedia to explore accommodations, compare prices, and read reviews. These platforms provide user-friendly interfaces to streamline the booking process.

Crafting your perfect stay in Kiwi paradise involves exploring diverse accommodation options. Whether opting for the luxury of a hotel, the sociable ambiance of a hostel, or the quirkiness of a unique stay, New Zealand's accommodations cater to every taste and budget. With careful planning and consideration of your preferences, your chosen accommodation becomes an integral part of your Kiwi adventure, ensuring a restful and delightful experience in this captivating destination.

Sustainable Travel

As explorers, our journeys extend beyond mere passages through landscapes; they present opportunities to connect with and safeguard the allure of our planet. In the enchanting realm of New Zealand, renowned for its unspoiled nature, adopting sustainable travel practices transcends mere choice – it evolves into a profound responsibility. In this exploration of sustainable travel, we will delve into eco-conscious methods and provide tips for responsible tourism, ensuring our imprints on this Kiwi paradise are tender and nurturing.

Eco-Friendly Practices

Reverence for Nature:
The landscapes of New Zealand, from the splendors of Fiordland National Park to the wonders of the Abel Tasman Coastal Track, are treasures deserving the utmost respect. Stick to designated trails, adhere to Leave No Trace principles, and refrain from disturbing wildlife. By immersing ourselves in nature without leaving a trace, we contribute to the preservation of these delicate ecosystems.

Sustainable Lodgings:
Choose accommodations that prioritize sustainability. Seek out hotels and lodges with eco-certifications, powered by renewable energy, and equipped with water and energy conservation measures. Alternatively, opt for eco-friendly lodgings like sustainable cabins or retreats seamlessly integrated into the surrounding environment.

Champion Local and Sustainable Cuisine:
Embark on a culinary journey through New Zealand, emphasizing local and sustainable choices. Select eateries that responsibly source ingredients, supporting local farmers and reducing the carbon footprint of your meals. Embrace the farm-to-table ethos, relishing the freshness of Kiwi produce.

Minimize Single-Use Plastics:
New Zealand's commitment to environmental preservation aligns with the global drive to reduce single-use plastics. Carry a reusable water bottle, reject plastic straws, and cut down on packaging waste. Through conscious choices, you contribute to a cleaner and healthier environment.

Low-Impact Transportation:
Explore New Zealand's breathtaking landscapes with minimal environmental impact. Opt for eco-friendly transportation such as electric or hybrid vehicles or utilize public transit. Consider guided eco-tours adhering to sustainable practices, minimizing the ecological footprint of your travels.

Participate in Conservation Initiatives:
Leave a positive impact by engaging in conservation activities. Numerous organizations and wildlife sanctuaries in New Zealand provide opportunities for visitors to contribute to habitat restoration, wildlife monitoring, and other initiatives. Active participation transforms you into a guardian of the land you explore.

Responsible Tourism Tips

Cultural Respect:
Celebrate the rich cultural heritage of New Zealand with reverence and sensitivity. Learn about Maori traditions and customs, engaging with local communities with an open heart. Seek permission before entering sacred sites, acknowledging the cultural significance of the places you visit.

Back Local Communities:
Opt for locally-owned businesses and support community initiatives. Whether acquiring crafts from local artisans or dining in family-owned establishments, your contributions directly enrich the communities you encounter. Interaction with locals fosters cultural exchange and deepens your travel experience.

Mindful Wildlife Encounters:
New Zealand shelters unique and vulnerable wildlife, including the kiwi bird and Hector's dolphin. When observing wildlife, maintain a respectful distance and avoid disrupting their natural behavior. Choose wildlife experiences prioritizing conservation and adhering to ethical guidelines.

Minimize Your Carbon Footprint:
Consider the environmental impact of your travels and take steps to minimize your carbon footprint. Offset emissions through reputable programs, choose direct flights when feasible, and explore carbon-neutral transportation. Mindful consideration of your ecological impact contributes to New Zealand's natural wonders' preservation.

Educate Yourself:

Knowledge is a potent tool for responsible tourism. Educate yourself about New Zealand's ecosystems, flora, and fauna. Understand the conservation challenges facing the country and actively seek opportunities to make positive contributions. Awareness deepens your connection to the land and its preservation.

Leave No Trace:

The "Leave No Trace" principle is paramount in responsible tourism. Pack out all waste, dispose of litter properly, and avoid activities that may harm the environment. By leaving no trace, you ensure that future generations can revel in the pristine beauty of New Zealand.

In nurturing New Zealand's natural wonders responsibly, sustainable travel transforms into a collective commitment to preserving the essence of this Kiwi paradise. By embracing eco-conscious practices and adhering to responsible tourism guidelines, travelers become pivotal in safeguarding the landscapes, cultures, and biodiversity defining New Zealand's allure. With each gentle step on Kiwi soil, the legacy of responsible travel unfolds, creating a harmonious balance between exploration and conservation.

Useful Resources

Embarking on a journey through the enchanting landscapes of New Zealand is more than a mere exploration; it entails tapping into invaluable resources to elevate your experience. Below, we have curated a compilation of essential aids that will assist you in orchestrating, navigating, and immersing yourself in the marvels of the Kiwi paradise.

Tourism New Zealand Hub:
Delve into a wealth of information on the official Tourism New Zealand website. From detailed destination guides and travel itineraries to essential safety tips and cultural insights, this comprehensive resource stands as your ultimate guide for meticulously planning every facet of your Kiwi adventure.

Department of Conservation (DOC) Gateway:
For enthusiasts of the great outdoors, the Department of Conservation website is indispensable. Offering intricate details on hiking trails, camping sites, and conservation projects, it ensures you stay abreast of track conditions, permits, and wildlife encounters, facilitating a seamless exploration of New Zealand's natural wonders.

Weather Intelligence Platforms:
Given New Zealand's diverse weather patterns, staying informed is paramount. Platforms like MetService and Weather.com provide real-time forecasts, enabling you to pack judiciously and plan outdoor activities with precision.

Currency Conversion Tools:

To navigate New Zealand's currency landscape, which revolves around the New Zealand Dollar (NZD), consider utilizing currency converter apps or websites. Options such as XE Currency and OANDA offer real-time exchange rates, ensuring you remain budget-savvy throughout your travels.

Digital Navigators: Enhancing Your Kiwi Adventure in the Digital Epoch

CamperMate:
Tailored for road trippers, CamperMate is a comprehensive app that aids in locating campsites, petrol stations, and other amenities on your route. Additionally, it furnishes information on activities, attractions, and insights shared by fellow travelers.

Google Maps:
A quintessential navigation tool, Google Maps is indispensable for exploring New Zealand. It provides detailed maps, real-time traffic updates, and information on local businesses. Download offline maps for areas with limited connectivity.

BookMe:
Your digital ally for last-minute deals on activities, accommodations, and attractions, BookMe offers discounted options, making spontaneous adventures more accessible.

Rankers Camping NZ:
Tailored for camping enthusiasts, Rankers Camping NZ showcases campsites, holiday parks, and freedom camping spots. User reviews and ratings assist in choosing the perfect spot for a night under the stars.

Language basics

While English predominates in New Zealand, incorporating local language basics can add a charming layer to your interactions:

- Kia Ora: Hello / Greetings
- Haere Mai: Welcome
- Aroha: Love
- Whanau: Family
- Kai: Food
- Puku: Stomach / Belly
- Mate: Dead / To Die
- Pakaru: Broken

Learning these basics can forge connections with locals and enrich your cultural experience in New Zealand.

Packing Checklist:

Outdoor Essentials:

- Hiking boots
- Weather-appropriate clothing layers
- Waterproof jacket
- Hat and sunglasses
- Daypack for hikes
- Electronics:

Camera or smartphone for capturing memories

- Power bank for on-the-go charging
- Adapters for New Zealand's power outlets

Travel Documents:

- Passport and visa (if required)
- Travel insurance details
- Copies of important documents (stored digitally and physically)

Health and Safety:

- First aid kit
- Prescription medications
- Insect repellent and sunscreen
- Emergency contact information

Money and Banking:

- New Zealand Dollars (NZD)
- Debit/credit cards
- Currency converter app

Navigation Tools:

- Maps and guidebooks
- GPS or smartphone with navigation apps
- Car rental documents (if applicable)

Miscellaneous:

- Reusable water bottle
- Travel towel
- Snorkeling gear (for coastal adventures)
- Daypack for urban exploration

Cultural Considerations:

- Modest clothing for cultural sites
- Knowledge of local customs and etiquette
- Respectful behavior towards indigenous culture

By incorporating these indispensable resources, apps, language basics, and a meticulously curated packing list into your Kiwi adventure, you'll not only navigate the landscapes with ease but also submerge yourself in the essence of New Zealand's natural beauty and cultural opulence. Whether you're a nature aficionado, cultural explorer, or a blend of both, these tools will enhance every facet of your journey through the Kiwi paradise.

Map Of New Zealand

Conclusion

As your Kiwi escapade approaches its finale, it's a moment to contemplate the rich tapestry of encounters woven into the core of New Zealand. From the awe-inspiring vistas of Fiordland National Park to the lively urban pulse of Auckland, each instance has contributed to a voyage surpassing the mere tally of physical miles traversed. The culmination of your Kiwi adventure isn't a destination; rather, it marks a temporary halt in a narrative that will linger in your recollections and reverberate in the depths of your being.

Reflecting on Your Kiwi Adventure

Pause to consider the kaleidoscope of moments that have characterized your Kiwi journey. The whisper of leaves along the Abel Tasman Coastal Track, the fragrance of a Hangi feast in Rotorua, the embrace of Kiwi warmth in a local homestay—these are not isolated snapshots but rather the brushstrokes forming a dynamic canvas painted with the hues of revelation.

Reflect on the bonds established with fellow voyagers and locals alike. The shared narratives in a Queenstown pub, the laughter exchanged at a Milford Sound campsite, the nods of respect during a cultural exchange in a Maori marae—these interactions have woven a social fabric that transcends boundaries and backgrounds.

Contemplate the tranquility discovered in moments of solitude. The hush of a starlit night in Lake Tekapo, the gentle lap of waves in the Bay of

Islands, the reflective pause atop the Tongariro Alpine Crossing—these are the still points anchoring your Kiwi journey within the realm of personal introspection.

Share Your Experience

Your Kiwi sojourn isn't solely yours; it evolves into a legacy shared with those destined to tread in your footsteps. As you conclude this chapter, consider imparting your experiences to fellow wayfarers and future explorers. Whether through travel chronicles, social media snippets, or heartfelt dialogues, your tales contribute to the collective narrative of Kiwi paradise.

Detail the flavor of a Fergburger in Queenstown, the exhilaration of bungee jumping in Taupo, the soul-stirring rhythms of Maori haka—communicate the tastes, sensations, and emotions shaping your odyssey. Your words serve as a bridge, linking others to the enchantment of New Zealand and kindling the spark for their own adventure.

Share practical insights and advice that could prove beneficial to those venturing into Kiwi paradise. From the hidden treasures uncovered in local markets to the off-the-beaten-path trails leading to awe-inspiring vistas, your wisdom transforms into a guidebook for future explorers, weaving a tapestry of shared discovery.

As you bid adieu to New Zealand, acknowledge that the end of one adventure is but the prelude to countless others. The memories etched in the landscapes of Aotearoa will continue to murmur tales of exploration, beckoning you to return or inspiring others to embark on their Kiwi voyage.

In the closing act of your Kiwi expedition, the landscapes may recede from immediate view, but the spirit of New Zealand endures within your heart. It's a destination not confined to maps and coordinates; it's an encounter that transcends the constraints of time and space, leaving an enduring imprint on the canvas of your life. The conclusion of your Kiwi journey is merely a comma, a brief pause, in a narrative that unfolds with every step taken on the path of exploration.

Love from Author

I express my sincere gratitude to you for accompanying me on this virtual expedition into the captivating landscapes and lively culture of New Zealand. Composing these words has been a labor of passion, driven by the belief that every wanderer deserves a guide that not only imparts information but also sparks the flame of curiosity.

Embarking on a journey through Kiwi terrain transcends mere physical exploration; it extends an invitation to immerse oneself in a rich tapestry of experiences that define the very essence of Aotearoa. From the untamed beauty of Fiordland National Park to the cultural tapestry of Rotorua, my intent has been to breathe life into the enchantment of New Zealand within these pages.

I trust that this guide has functioned as a reliable companion, offering practical insights, cultural significance, and a touch of wanderlust to kindle your imagination. Whether you are a seasoned adventurer seeking fresh horizons or someone orchestrating their inaugural Kiwi odyssey, my hope is that these words act as a source of inspiration and guidance along your path.

As you embark on your personal odyssey, recognize that each footfall presents an opportunity to connect with the world, steep yourself in diverse cultures, and carve memories destined to endure long after the journey concludes. New Zealand, with its awe-inspiring landscapes and hospitable denizens, eagerly anticipates your exploration.

May your travels be punctuated with discovery, may the beauty you encounter uplift your spirit, and may the memories you cultivate be wellsprings of joy in the years ahead. Feel the gentle caress of the wind on your face while traversing the Abel Tasman Coastal Track, relish the flavors of Kiwi cuisine, and embrace the warmth of cultural exchanges.

Thank you for bestowing upon me a fragment of your travel narrative. May your Kiwi adventure unfold as nothing short of extraordinary, and may the stories woven along the way become cherished chapters in the narrative of your life.

Wishing you safe and exhilarating travels, intrepid souls!

Warm regards,

[**Amanda Fenner**]

[Author of "New Zealand Travel Guide 2024"]

Printed in Great Britain
by Amazon